STIRLING AND THE TROSSACHS
A pictorial souvenir

NESS PUBLISHING

2 Seen from Stirling Castle, the Wallace Monument stands tall on Abbey Craig against the backdrop of Dumyat, an outlier of the Ochil Hills.

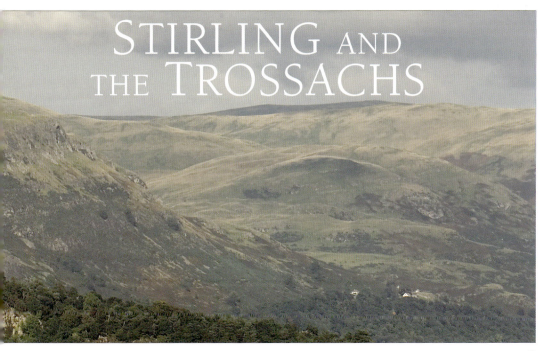

STIRLING AND THE TROSSACHS

Welcome to Stirling!

It is in this historic city that we shall begin an exploration throughout the district which nowadays bears that name, including that most famed region of Scottish hill country, The Trossachs. And The Trossachs lead down to the equally famous bonnie banks of Loch Lomond. Over the years boundaries have changed and the county (or District as it is now generally known) of Stirlingshire has gained territory, mostly from Perthshire, so the journey on which this book embarks takes in some places whose residents still feel a greater allegiance to their former county.

Stirling is the most strategically important site in Scotland, located in the heart of the country and poetically described as 'the brooch that holds the highlands and lowlands together'. Like Edinburgh, it is perched on a volcanic plug from which the surrounding area can be surveyed and controlled. It is also situated at what used to be the lowest bridging point of the River Forth which rises away to the west in The Trossachs.

Stirling Castle's site has been occupied since prehistoric times. First mention of the castle itself goes back to the reign of Alexander I (1107-1124), but how long it existed before that is not known. Given Stirling's strategic value, it is no surprise that it has seen some of the most significant battles in Scotland's history. The two most notable were the Battle of Stirling Bridge in 1297 when William Wallace led the Scots to victory over the English, and Robert the Bruce's

A view down Loch Lomond from Inversnaid on the eastern side of the loch. By area, this is the largest freshwater loch in Britain, stretching 24 miles from Balloch in the south to Ardlui in the north.

more lasting success at Bannockburn in 1314. Following these two defeats of the English, it is a sad irony that the Battle of Sauchieburn (very close to Bannockburn) in 1488 found members of the Scottish royal family on opposite sides: James III's own son joined the rebels. The King left the battle but was slain soon afterwards and his rebel son duly became James IV. James III and his Queen, Margaret of Denmark, are both buried at Cambuskenneth Abbey, just across the Forth from Stirling (opposite).

During the 15th and 16th centuries Stirling Castle's role gradually changed from military stronghold to royal residence, a symbol of the Stewart dynasty's power. This was most lavishly expressed in the construction of a French-style palace completed around 1540, during the reign of James V. In 1566 Mary, Queen of Scots, used the castle as the backdrop for a celebration of the baptism of her son, the future King James VI. Yet soldiers continued to be quartered there until 1964. Stirling's old town, running down the tail of the volcanic plug, is full of historic buildings, many of which have medieval origins. If these walls could speak, what tales they could tell! Several of them do continue to tell their story to visitors, such as Argyll's Lodging, Holy Rude Church and the Old Town Jail.

This area is not short of innovation either: a few miles away to the south is Falkirk, home of the Falkirk Wheel, the world's first and only rotating boat lift. The Wheel was the visionary solution to the problem of restoring the missing link between the Forth & Clyde Canal and the Union Canal. Historically, the two canals had been joined at Falkirk by a flight of 11 locks, but these were dismantled in 1933. Now the Falkirk Wheel lifts boats 35m/115ft, the height difference between the two canals.

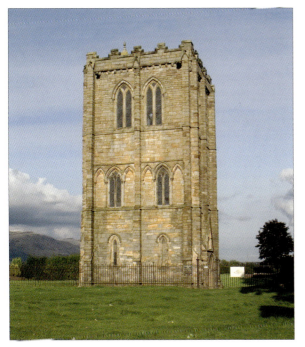 

Left: Cambuskenneth Abbey. Right: An aerial view of the Falkirk Wheel.
The completion of this project was marked by Her Majesty The Queen on 24 May 2002.

8 Stirling's old town forms an impressive silhouette against the evening light. The castle occupies most of the right-hand side, while to the left the towers of Holy Rude Church and the Old Town Jail stand

out. Stirling heritage dates back 800 years to the 12th century, when the town first received the burgh title. It was granted a Royal Charter, becoming one of the most important towns of medieval Scotland.

10 This view of the western side of Stirling Castle clearly shows what a defensible site it is. Nevertheless, it was not immune from stone-throwing siege engines.

From the gentler slope to the south, the castle is bristling with bastions and gun emplacements. The Great Hall (right of centre) has been restored in recent years and returned to its limewashed finish.

12 The Outer Close of the castle, with the guns of the Grand Battery trained to the east and the Main Guard House beyond.

And now, looking towards the Grand Battery from the Wallace Monument, early morning sun picks out the Great Hall, built by James IV during the years 1501 to 1504.

14 From the Outer Defences of the castle, Robert the Bruce (r. 1306-1329) surveys his domain. The 67m/220ft high Wallace Monument can be seen in the distance on Abbey Craig.

 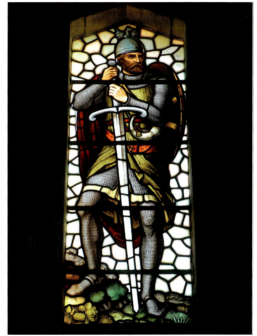

Left: the Wallace Monument in close-up. It was from this hilltop in 1297 that William Wallace watched the English Army approach Stirling Bridge. Right: The William Wallace window at the monument.

16 Just down from the castle, Argyll's Lodging is the best and most complete surviving example of a 17th-century Scottish townhouse. The conical turrets demonstrate French influence.

Cowane's Hospital, built between 1639 and 1649. John Cowane, a wealthy Stirling merchant, bequeathed funds for its construction. It originally offered charity to unsuccessful merchants.

18 The Church of the Holy Rude, where John Knox preached, Mary, Queen of Scots worshipped and James VI was crowned. Founded in 1129, it is the second oldest building in Stirling.

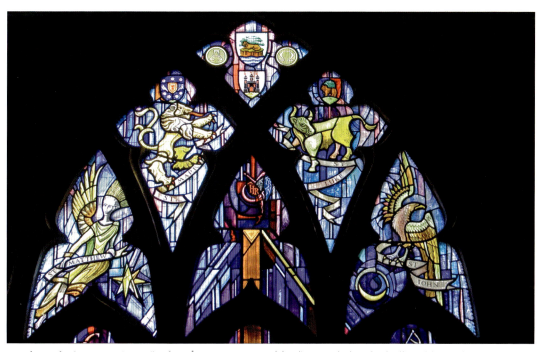

Holy Rude (meaning 'cross') Church contains a wealth of stained glass including this modern piece, the Guildry Window, which was donated in 1993. This picture shows the detail of its upper part.

20 A scene that captures the character of Stirling's old town, looking from Holy Rude Churchyard with the Tolbooth clock tower in the distance. The Tolbooth was reopened as an arts centre in 2002.

A fine array of townhouses in Broad Street. The tall one in the centre of the picture is traditionally said to have been the home of Lord Darnley, first husband of Mary, Queen of Scots.

22 The imposing structure of The Old Town Jail. It received its first prisoners in 1847. Though the regime was harsh, the accommodation was a big improvement on earlier prisons.

 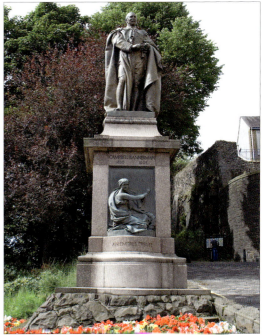

Left: a visit to the Jail today will bring you face to face with some of its past personalities.
Right: statue of Campbell Bannerman, MP for the burgh and Prime Minister from 1905-1908.

24 This downhill view shows how the old town descends to the new. The limewashed building on the left is Spittal's House, established as an almshouse in the 16th century.

Left: statue of Rob Roy MacGregor, one of Scotland's greatest folk heroes, in Dumbarton Road.
Right: a few yards away, Scotland's greatest poet, Robert Burns, keeps watch.

26 Stirling Old Bridge, built around 1500. It succeeded earlier structures, including the wooden bridge where Sir William Wallace defeated the English at the Battle of Stirling Bridge in 1297.

From one great battle site to another: the Battle of Bannockburn took place on 24th June 1314. Robert the Bruce's victory over the English is commemorated in this statue and cairn (inset).

28 We now leave Stirling and head west across the south of the District. This is the charming village of Fintry – the house used to be Stewart's School, built 1859. The Fintry hills rise behind.

Stirling's southern boundary runs through The Campsie Fells, a ridge of hills that runs east-west for several miles. They are seen here from near the village of Balfron as the sun goes down.

30 Continuing west we reach the pretty village of Killearn. The column seen through the trees commemorates renowned scholar George Buchanan, 1506-1582, who was born here.

This picture shows Killearn's fine location under the western end of the Campsie Fells – the village is visible on the left, halfway up the picture.

32 The Endrick Water takes run-off from the Fintry Hills and the Campsie Fells into Loch Lomond. On its way it flows past the village of Drymen where it is crossed by this bridge.

These beautifully frosted trees are also in the vicinity of Drymen.

34 Morning mist creates an ethereal scene over Loch Lomond, with the snowy summit of Ben Lomond (974m/3195ft) towering above.

Stirling's western boundary runs down the middle of Loch Lomond, so villages on the eastern side belong to the District. One such is Balmaha, from where this sunset view was recorded.

36 Contrasting light effects seen at Balmaha boatyard, showing another of Loch Lomond's many moods. The West Highland Way passes through Balmaha on its route from Milngavie to Fort William.

North of Balmaha and close to Loch Lomond lies the Dubh ('black') Lochan. Being sheltered and relatively small it can provide stunning reflections of the surrounding terrain.

38 The usual starting point for climbing Ben Lomond is Rowardennan at the end of the road up the east bank of Loch Lomond. From the ascent is seen this inviting landscape of heather and waterfalls.

The view east from Ben Lomond, looking across the summit corrie down to distant Loch Ard (see p.68). Ben Lomond is the most southerly of Scotland's 284 Munros (hills above 914m/3000ft).

40 And to the west, spectacular lighting adds drama to the mountainscape on the far side of Loch Lomond. The further stretch of water is the head of Loch Long. These hills are known

as the Arrochar Alps and will feature in more detail in the Argyll title in this series of books.

42 Now it's time to leave Loch Lomond behind and head north up Glen Falloch, where the lovely Falls of Falloch await inspection.

A few miles further on brings travellers to Crianlarich, where the train disembarks a party of young adventurers. The railway divides here, with one line going to Oban and the other to Fort William.

44 The north-western corner of Stirling District is the location of its highest mountains. Overlooking Crianlarich, Ben More (1174m/3852ft) and Stob Binnein (1165m/3822ft) catch the evening sun.

Presenting an equally wintry but very different aspect, Ben Lui (1130m/3707ft) is sometimes described as the 'Queen of Scottish mountains' and sits on the western edge of Stirling District.

46 Even on a dull day a calm loch can provide captivating scenes. Having turned east to continue our circular tour, this is Loch Lubhair at the head of Glen Dochart.

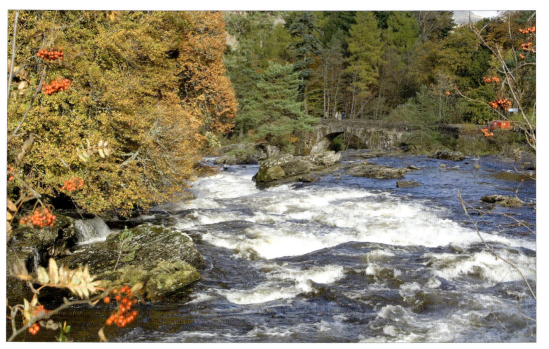

About ten miles downstream, the waters from Loch Lubhair cascade through the village of Killin at the Falls of Dochart. There is much more to see in Killin, including views down Loch Tay.

48 South from Killin, the next stop is Lochearnhead. This area used to belong to Perthshire; St Fillans, 6.5 miles away at the other end of Loch Earn, remains in that county (see *Perthshire* in this series).

Edinample Castle, built in the late 16th century and perhaps incorporating parts of an earlier structure, enjoys glorious views over Loch Earn.

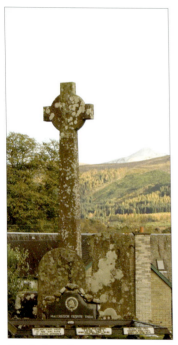 

50 Left: Rob Roy MacGregor's grave in Balquhidder churchyard with Ben Vorlich in the distance.
Right: Beyond Balquhidder to the west, a storm brews over Loch Voil.

Only about three miles south from Lochearnhead, we are now in the northern Trossachs.
The storm having passed, Loch Voil is bathed in soft evening light…

52 ...while in the opposite direction the setting sun creates silhouettes in the afterglow.

The Braes of Balquhidder line the north side of Loch Voil. The autumn bracken is given extra brilliance by the low evening light.

54 Continuing south, through Strathyre, Loch Lubnaig is the next reason to pause. Across the loch to the west the slopes of Ben Ledi rise to an early covering of snow on the higher reaches.

Climbing Ben Ledi gives a different perspective on Loch Lubnaig, while about 20 miles away to the north, winter has come early to Ben Lawers (1214m/3983ft).

56 The whole of The Trossachs can be surveyed from the top of Ben Ledi (879m/2885ft). Mountains in this height range (between 762m/2500ft and 914m/3000ft) are classified as 'Corbetts', as identified by

John Rooke Corbett. There are approximately 220 in Scotland. The woodland on the eastern slopes of Ben Ledi forms part of the Queen Elizabeth Forest Park which covers numerous tracts of The Trossachs.

58 The westward view from Ben Ledi overlooks Glen Finglas ('glen of white water') which, since 1955, has contained the reservoir named Loch Finglas, seen in the foreground.

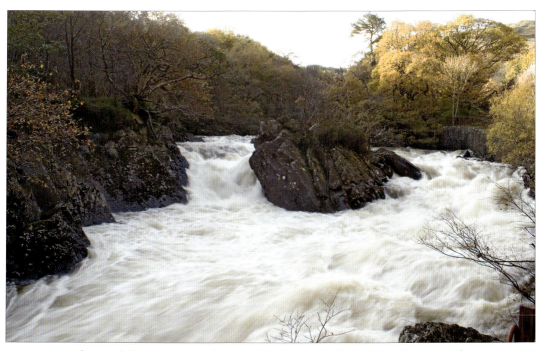

A mile or so below the outflow from Loch Lubnaig, the Garbh Uisge (appropriately meaning 'rough water') crashes through the Falls of Leny, close by the A84.

60 And now towards the heart of The Trossachs: heading west, the expanse of Loch Venachar (a reservoir) leads to the hills beyond, with Ben Venue (727m/2386ft) in the distance.

For some, this spot epitomises The Trossachs: Loch Achray is set amidst a ring of hills whose changing seasonal colours constantly renew the scene. (See also front cover)

62 'Trossachs' comes from the Gaelic 'troisichean' meaning a small glen that joins two larger glens. Trossachs Glen, just a mile or so long, connects the wider spaces of Loch Achray and Loch Katrine, above.

Loch Katrine is a reservoir based on a natural loch which has had its water level raised. Seen from a boat on the loch, Ellen's Isle is in the foreground with the north shores of the loch behind.

64 The SS Sir Walter Scott has plied Loch Katrine from Trossachs Pier at its eastern extremity to Stronachlachar since 1900.

Having returned from Loch Katrine, here is the classic view of Loch Achray, with the former Achray Hotel (now time-share apartments) looking imposing and giving scale to the view.

66 From Achray we go south over Duke's Pass through more of the Queen Elizabeth Forest Park, pausing to take in the contrasting characters of Ben A'an (right) and snowy Stob a' Choin in the distance.

The Forestry Commission's David Marshall Visitor Centre is at the southern end of the Duke's Pass, above the town of Aberfoyle. This lochan is one of the features at the centre.

68 Westwards from Aberfoyle, we find the tranquillity of Loch Ard with its perfect view of Ben Lomond. This area was the site of a fierce battle in 711.

Continuing, now north-west, the next stretch of water is secluded Loch Chon. From here, the road takes you via Loch Arklet to its terminus at Inversnaid – the location pictured on p.5.

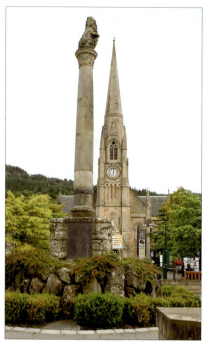 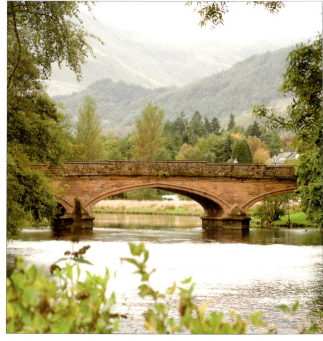

70 The town of Callander (formerly in Perthshire) is a good centre for exploring The Trossachs. Above left is Ancaster Square with the Rob Roy Centre in the church building; right: Callander Bridge.

The tranquil remains of Inchmahome Priory, an Augustinian monastery dating from 1238, now in the care of Historic Scotland. It sheltered the child Mary, Queen of Scots in 1547.

72 The priory is situated on an island in the middle of the Lake of Menteith, a few miles south of Callander. Visitors are conveyed to the island in boats like this one.

Sunset over the Lake of Menteith. It is Scotland's only 'lake'; its name may have arisen from a misunderstanding of the Gaelic word 'laich' meaning a low-lying area.

74 An eastwards shift brings us to the village of Doune and its magnificent late 14th-century castle. Inset: a musket-firing demonstration at one of Doune Castle's historical re-enactment events.

Architecturally important cottages in George Street, Doune, designed by the expatriate Scots architect Thomas MacLaren and completed in 1894.

76 A further eastwards hop and we reach Dunblane, where this unusual and attractive town name-board and signpost greets travellers at the Perth Road roundabout.

From Dunblane High Street, with the Leighton Library on the left. It was built in 1687 as the result of a bequest by Robert Leighton, Bishop of Dunblane from 1661 to 1670.

78 Dunblane Cathedral Close, with the Cathedral Museum on the right. The picture of the Cathedral on the back of this book was taken from the steps leading to the first floor door of the museum.

Inside Dunblane Cathedral: left, an etched-glass Celtic cross; centre, the organ; right, memorial to the tragic events of 1996. Today the Cathedral is home to a congregation of 1200 worshippers.

Published 2009 by Ness Publishing, 47 Academy Street, Elgin, Moray, IV30 1LR
Phone/fax 01343 549663 www.nesspublishing.co.uk

All photographs © Colin and Eithne Nutt except p.7 (right) © Scotavia Images; p.15 (right) © National Wallace Monument;
p.23 (left) © Stirling Old Town Jail; pp.33-37, 42 & 44 © Les Davidson; p.64 © The Steamship Sir Walter Scott Limited.
Text © Colin Nutt

ISBN 978-1-906549-07-7

All rights reserved. No part of this publication may be reproduced, stored in a retrieval system, in any form or by any means, without prior permission of Ness Publishing. The right of Colin Nutt as author of this work has been asserted by him in accordance with the Copyright, Designs and Patents Act 1988.

Front cover: (main) Loch Achray (insets) two of the 'Stirling Heads'; p.1: Mar's Wark, Stirling;
p.4: roof detail at Stirling Castle; this page: the Star Pyramid (a martyrs' memorial), Stirling; back cover: Dunblane Cathedral

For a list of websites and phone numbers please turn over >

Websites and phone numbers (where available) in the order they appear in this book:

Stirling: www.stirling.co.uk
Loch Lomond: www.loch-lomond.net
Loch Lomond & Trossachs National Park: www.lochlomond-trossachs.org (T) 01389 722600
Cambuskenneth Abbey: www.historic-scotland.gov.uk
Falkirk Wheel: www.thefalkirkwheel.co.uk (T) 01324 619888
Stirling Castle: www.historic-scotland.gov.uk (T) 01786 450000
National Wallace Monument: www.nationalwallacemonument.com (T) 01786 472140
Argyll's Lodging: www.historic-scotland.gov.uk (T) 01786 450000
Cowane's Hospital: www.instirling.com
Church of the Holy Rude www.holyrude.org
Old Town Jail: www.oldtownjail.com (T) 01786 450050
Stirling Old Bridge www.instirling.com
Bannockburn: www.nts.org.uk (T) 0844 493 2139
Campsie Fells: www.geo.ed.ac.uk
Balfron: www.balfron.org.uk
Killearn: www.killearn.org.uk
Drymen: www.drymen.com
Balmaha: www.loch-lomond.net/villages
Crianlarich Station: www.nationalrail.co.uk/stations
Killin: www.killin.co.uk
Breadalbane Folklore Centre: www.breadalbanefolklorecentre.com (T) 01567 820254
Lochearnhead and Edinample Castle: www.perthshire-scotland.co.uk